ALEX

MURDAUG

H'S CASE

THE REAL

STORY

By

Jerry F. Stack

TABLE OF CONTENTS

Introduction

- Alex Murdaugh's Biography

- Alex Murdaugh's Career

- **Alex Murdaugh's Personal Life**

- **Mallory Beach's Death**

- **Alex Murdaugh's Arrest And Crime Cases**

• Alex Murdaugh's Trial and Verdict

INTRODUCTION.

A South Carolina lawyer named Alex Murdaugh was found guilty of killing his wife Maggie, 52, and son Paul, 22, and was given a life sentence.

Murdaugh, a disbarred 54-year-old attorney, was found guilty on two counts of murder in the June 2021 killings as well as two counts of possessing a weapon while committing a violent crime. He was sentenced in Judge Clifton Newman's court.

Alex Murdaugh responded, "I would never hurt Maggie and I would never hurt Paul," when asked if he had killed or would ever hurt his son or wife.

Key episodes in Alex Murdaugh's trial were violence,

corruption, and power.

After less than three hours of deliberation on March 3,2023, the jury returned a guilty judgment, ending the six-week trial that had gripped the nation and the rest of the globe with its intricate web of murder, power, and corruption.

Alex Murdaugh's Biography.

Alex Murdaugh was born on the 17th day of June 1968 in South Carolina. For some who may not be aware, Alex Murdaugh comes from a family that is well known in the legal calling as his great granddad, granddad, and father were all legal advisors.

Alex Murdaugh was a student at Hampton High School where he obtained a BA in Political Science from the University of South Carolina and in 1994, a legal degree from the University of Carolina School of Law.

Alex Murdaugh was called to the South Carolina Bar as at November 1994 and has been a practicing lawyer ever since then.

Alex Murdaugh and his late wife Maggie met each other and started dating in college while attending the University of South Carolina.
Both of them got married on August

14, 1993, in South Carolina and welcomed their first child and son Richard Alexander Buster Murdaugh three years later before Paul was born. Paul was a law student at the University of South Carolina before his death.

Alex Murdaugh's Career.

Alex Murdaugh began his legal career at the Peters, Murdaugh, Parker, Eltzroth, and Detrick law firm (PMPED),which was founded by his great-grandfather in 1910 and remains one of the most well-respected law firms in the state.

In recent years, Murdaugh has also worked as a part-time prosecutor in the 14th Circuit Solicitor's Office which prosecutes criminal cases over five counties – since 1920.

Alex's great-grandfather, grandfather Randolph Murdaugh Jr, and father Randolph Murdaugh III worked the same office until 2006.

However, the law firm went through a restructuring in January 2022 after Alex faced legal problems, resulting in the current name The Parker Law Group.

Alex Murdaugh worked for his family's law firm

until September 3, 2021, when he was forced out of the firm for stealing millions of dollars from the firm and its clients, leading him to resign from his position.

Since 2014, Alex Murdaugh and other members of the

Murdaugh family have been actively involved in investigations involving several murders, corruption, and other alleged crimes, including insurance fraud, defrauding clients, theft of insurance payouts, and drug-related charges.

Alex Murdaugh's Personal Life.

Alex Murdaugh's personal life has been marked by lots of tragedies and notorious crimes.

Alex Murdaugh struggled with an

addiction to opioids for the last 20 years when he was spending $50,000 per week to support his habit. Despite making millions, he allegedly stole millions from his law firm to support his habit

Following that the most tragic event where Alex Murdaugh really saw his downfall was the infamous boat accident that killed Mallory Beach.

Despite these personal shortcomings, Alex Murdaugh remained

steadfast in legal and political circles in the state. He served as a member of the South Carolina Bar Association and has been involved in various political campaigns over the years until his arrest which led to him being disbarred.

The Death of Mallory Beach.

At roughly 2:20 a.m. on February 24, 2019, Paul Terry Murdaugh crashed his family boat into the Archers Creek Bridge in Beaufort, South Carolina. On board the boat at the hour of the accident were Mallory Beach and a few different youngsters.

Mallory Beach was killed in the accident and Murdaugh was charged comparable to the accident.

On April 18, 1999, in Walterboro, South

Carolina, Phillip Harley and Renee Searson Beach had a daughter, Mallory Madison Beach. She had attended Wade Hampton Secondary School. The 19-year-old was working at a fashion shop and attending school at the time of her death.

In the minutes before the incident, Paul Murdaugh used his brother's identification to buy alcohol at a convenience shop in Ridgeland, South Carolina.

Three couples, including Beach and her boyfriend and

Murdaugh and his girlfriend, got on a speed boat and headed to an oyster roast after meeting at the home of Murdaugh's grandpa on the Chechesee River.

They made a halt in Beaufort at a dockside pub around

one o'clock the afternoon for Murdaugh and another passenger to take shots.

Murdaugh started acting strangely, and even when other passengers pleaded with him to let someone else steer the boat, he refused.

The boat struck a piling on the Parris Island bridge about 2:20 in the afternoon.

Except for Mallory Beach's boyfriend, who insisted on sticking behind to wait for word about Mallory Beach, the other passengers were taken to a local hospital after the accident.

Volunteers and investigators looked for Mallory Beach for eight days. Two volunteers discovered her remains on March 3, 2019, roughly five miles downstream from the crash site. Beach died from a combination of trauma and drowning.

Paul, who was operating the boat, his brother, who is accused of lending the minor Paul his license so that he could purchase alcohol, and Paul's mother Maggie, who is accused of permitting Paul to operate the boat while intoxicated, are all named in a lawsuit brought by Mallory Beach's mother Renee Beach.

The lawsuit, which was resolved in

January 2023, also implicated Alex Murdaugh and the store where the minors purchased the alcohol. Several Murdaugh family members, the hosts of the oyster roast, the owner of the bar where Murdaugh took shots following the oyster roast, and the owner of the convenience store where Murdaugh purchased alcohol were all named in lawsuits filed by Renee Beach.

Three felonies, including drunken boating and drunken boating that resulted in death, were leveled against Paul Murdaugh. Paul entered a not guilty plea and was granted bond.

Paul and his mother Maggie were killed on June 7, 2021, and the now-deceased Paul was not prosecuted.

On July 15, 2022, his father, Alex Murdaugh, was charged with murder and convicted after a jury trial.

Alex Murdaugh's Arrest And Crime Cases.

Murdaugh was Arrested and found guilty of murder in the deaths of his wife and son after around six weeks of testimony in the double murder trial, which started in January.

Below is a timeline of significant events in the case.

On June 7, 2021

At 10:07 p.m., Murdaugh calls 911

to report that he has discovered Margaret and Paul's lifeless bodies close to the family's dog kennels on their hunting lodge estate in rural Colleton County.

Murdaugh tells a dispatcher, his voice trembling, "I've been gone. "I just returned,"

June 10, 2021

Murdaugh's father, Randolph Murdaugh III, passes away at home in Hampton County, South Carolina at the age of 81 following a number of medical issues. His passing, however unrelated to the killings, heightens the mystery surrounding the case.

June 14, 2021

Margaret and Paul each had several gunshot wounds, according to a coroner, and their deaths were predicted to occur between 9:00 and 9:30 p.m.

September 4, 2021

Murdaugh is hurt in a roadside shooting in Hampton County according to officials.

Jim Griffin, his friend and attorney, tells news organizations that Murdaugh pulled over his black Mercedes-Benz SUV because it had a flat tire when a pickup truck drove by, turned around, and someone inside started shooting.

Sept. 5, 2021

Murdaugh was transported to Memorial Health University Medical Center in Savannah, Georgia, for treatment, according to the authorities, who describe his injuries as a "superficial" head wound.

On September 6, 2021

Murdaugh issues a public statement in which he admits that he "made a lot of mistakes that he sincerely regrets" and that he has left his family's legal company in order to enter rehab.

A few hours later, his company, Peters, Murdaugh, Parker, Eltzroth & Detrickhe, issues a statement of its own in which it accuses Murdaugh of embezzling company funds.

Sept. 8, 2021

The South Carolina Supreme Court permanently revokes Alex Murdaugh's right to practice law.

Sept. 14, 2021

Authorities reveals fresh information about the incident on the highway. In order for his older son, Buster, to be able to collect on a $10 million life insurance policy, they claim that Murdaugh set up a guy to kill him. Curtis Edward Smith, 61, has been detained on suspicion of assisting suicide, assault and battery of a very aggravating nature, brandishing a firearm, insurance fraud, and conspiracy to commit insurance fraud.

Sept. 16, 2021

After being accused of insurance fraud, conspiring to conduct insurance fraud, and making a fraudulent police report, Murdaugh turns himself in to the authorities.

A court grants him bond, requires him

to give up his passport, but allows him to go back to a drug recovery facility.

On October 14, 2021

Murdaugh is detained in Florida after leaving a drug rehabilitation center. Following a probe into millions of dollars that vanished from a settlement related to the death of Satterfield, authorities accuse him of two felonies of obtaining property under false pretenses.

Her heirs claim that none of the $4.3

million settlement,
which they claim
was arranged
covertly by
Murdaugh, went to
them.

Oct. 19, 2021

A court in South
Carolina refuses

Murdaugh bond and
requires him to get a

mental health
assessment.

Nov. 19, 2021

New indictments
totaling 27 counts
have been
announced against
Murdaugh as a
result of the state's
investigation into his
business dealings;

they include forgery, money laundering, computer crimes, breach of trust with fraudulent intent, obtaining a signature or property under false pretenses, and breach of trust with fraudulent intent.

Dec. 9, 2021

Further charges, including nine counts of trust breach with fraudulent intent, seven counts of computer crimes, four counts of money laundering, and one act of forgery, are announced by the attorney general.

Murdaugh is accused of 48 distinct offenses in total. Prosecutors claim that the victims include close family friends, an undocumented immigrant, and a guy involved in a car accident.

Dec. 13, 2021

Murdaugh's bond is set by the judge at $7 million. For the first time in months, Murdaugh, who is being held in the Richland County jail, addresses the court.

He claims that when he attempted to kill himself in September, he was experiencing opiate withdrawal.

Alex Murdaugh claims, "My head is on straighter, and I'm thinking clearer than I have in a long, long time.

Jan. 21, 2022

Murdaugh is charged by a grand jury with 23 new offenses, including computer crimes and breach of trust with fraudulent purpose. He is accused of stealing nearly $8.5 million over the course of 71 separate offenses.

Jan. 24, 2022

The mother of Mallory Beach, 19, who died in a boat accident in 2019, has brought a lawsuit against the estates of Margaret and Paul Murdaugh.

Investigators claim that Paul was the boat's captain at some point during the night of underage drinking with six people on board.

The 18 to 20-year-old passengers were

thrown off the boat
when it collided with
a piling beneath a
bridge.

In an effort to obtain
the compensation
they feel they are
due as a result of the
accident, two
survivors join the

Beach family's court action.

March 16, 2022

Murdaugh is charged by a grand jury with four new offenses in connection with an insurance fraud plan involving Cory

Fleming, a friend
and another lawyer.

In a statement,
Fleming's attorney
claims that his client
is "yet another
casualty of the
multitude of crimes
committed by Alex
Murdaugh."

May 4, 2022

Four fresh charges
against Murdaugh
for financial crimes
that also involved
Fleming and others
are made public by
the prosecution.

June 24, 2022

A new set of charges
against Smith, a
friend of Alex

Murdaugh, includes four counts of money laundering, three counts of forgery, and criminal conspiracy. Smith was arrested.

June 28, 2022

Murdaugh and Smith are charged by a grand jury with

criminal conspiracy and drug charges. Smith has already been charged with other narcotics offenses. The guys are charged with planning to buy and sell oxycodone in Colleton County between October 7, 2013, and September 7, 2021.

July 13, 2022

Murdaugh is officially disbarred by the South Carolina Supreme Court despite being the subject of 11 lawsuits and 84 criminal complaints.

July 14, 2022

Murdaugh has been charged with two counts of double murder in the murders of Margaret and Paul, according to a grand jury's announcement.

According to two people familiar with the investigation, there is cellphone video that officials believe not only shows Murdaugh at the crime scene just before it happened but also deviates from an earlier account of what happened on the day of the deaths.

In a statement, Murdaugh's

attorneys claim that it was obvious from the start that police enforcement and the Attorney General wrongly believed that Alex Murdaugh was guilty of the deaths of his wife and son. Nonetheless, we are aware that Alex had no reason to murder them at all.

July 20, 2022

Alex Murdaugh pleads not guilty on the counts of murder.

Aug. 19, 2022

Murdaugh is charged by a grand

jury with nine more offenses linked to computer fraud and money laundering.

In late 2020 and early 2021, the indictment claims, Murdaugh stole money from his company.

It also claims that in 2017–2018, he took

advantage of a mistake made by the company's accounting department, which sent him $121,358 for a loan repayment when it should have gone to his brother.

Oct. 13, 2022

The Colleton County Courthouse will host Murdaugh's murder trial on January 23 according to the state Attorney General's Office. The trial is anticipated to go on for over three weeks.

Dec. 9, 2022

State prosecutors asserted during a pretrial hearing that Murdaugh killed his wife and son in an effort to win sympathy and "avoid the blame" for a series of financial misdeeds.

The defense team for Murdaugh

disputes the state's justification and argues that he would not have "shifted a financial probe away from himself in order to evade scrutiny" before "becoming caught up in a murder investigation."

Dec. 16, 2022

Murdaugh is charged by a grand jury with nine counts of tax evasion on the grounds that he failed to pay almost $487,000 in state income taxes over the course of nine years while earning close to $14 million. The most recent indictment brings Murdaugh's total number of financial-related counts to more than 100.

Dec. 20, 2022

At Murdaugh's double murder trial, state prosecutors

declare that they will push for life in prison without the possibility of parole, sparing him the possibility of being executed.

Jan. 23, 2023

Jury selection begins the Murdaugh double murder trial

at the Colleton
County Courthouse.

Jan. 25, 2023

State prosecutors
claim in their
opening statement
that Murdaugh used
a shotgun and an
AR-style rifle to kill
his wife and son at
close range and that

forensic evidence would establish his guilt.

The prosecution's case, the defense asserts in its opening statement, is riddled with flaws and rests on "theories" and "conjectures," according to the defense.

Feb. 1, 2023

Three voices can be heard in the background of a previously unknown video played by the prosecution that was shot from Paul Murdaugh's phone just before the killings take place.

Witnesses swear that the voices belong to Alex, Paul, and Margaret. This implicates the patriarch in the crime and calls into question his claim that he was not present when his wife and son were killed.

Feb. 23, 2023

Murdaugh testifies for himself during the fifth week of the trial. He admits, "I didn't shoot my wife or son," and as his lawyer asks him to explain the crime scene, he repeatedly sobs.

Feb. 24, 2023

Murdaugh is back in court. The prosecution questions him about his "new tale" during cross-examination, claiming that his earlier testimony was made up to fit with their video evidence showing he saw his wife and son minutes before they were discovered dead.

Murdaugh claims that because of his dependence on prescription painkillers and his general paranoia, he lied to law enforcement officials about where he was when the murders took place.

Alex Murdaugh's Trial and

Verdict

At the Colleton County Courthouse in Walterboro, South Carolina,

Murdaugh's trial got underway on January 25, 2023, with directions from the judge and opening statements from the prosecution and defense.

Jim Griffin and Dick Harpootlian acted as

Murdaugh's attorneys.

Clifton Newman, oversaw the cases.

The prosecution team against Murdaugh was led by state grand jury chief prosecutor Creighton Waters.

The South Carolina Attorney General

selected John Meadors, a Columbia lawyer with substantial expertise in murder prosecutions, to be a member of the prosecution team.

It was anticipated that both the defense and prosecution will call hundreds of witnesses.

Prosecutor Creighton Waters informed the jury during the opening statement of Alex Murdugh's trial on January 25, 2023, that Margaret and Paul's injuries were stated "as if they didn't sense a threat coming from their attacker."

Waters told the jury that the injuries were also "gruesome". He also made note of the cellphone data that showed Murdaugh arriving at the crime scene immediately before his family's phones "went silent forever". Within Murdaugh's parents' house, police also discovered a raincoat that was "wadded up" and "coated in gunshot residue."

Afterwards, Murdaugh revealed

on the witness stand that he had misled the police about his whereabouts the night of his family's killings.

When questioned if he had killed or would ever hurt his son or wife, Alex Murdaugh responded, "I would

never hurt Maggie
and I would never
hurt Paul."

Murdaugh
responded, "I would
never hurt Maggie
and I would never
hurt paul.

Defense counsel
argued that the
prosecution

shouldn't be allowed to ask questions about Murdaugh's financial crimes.

The judge overruled the defense attorney's objections and stated he would issue a formal ruling on the matter on Thursday, February 2, 2023.

On February 2, the judge preemptively excused the jury in Alex Murdaugh's ongoing trial so that the prosecution could call two witnesses to testify about Murdaugh's financial crimes at an in chambers session. Before deciding whether to allow these witnesses to testify to the jury, the judge stated that he needed to hear more testimony in private.

On February 7, following several days of hearing arguments without the jury present,

Judge Newman decided the testimony relating to Murdaugh's alleged financial crimes was admissible.

He stated that jurors were entitled to think about whether Murdaugh's financial situation was a reason for the killings. Additionally, according to Newman, when the defense team asked a witness to speculate on a potential reason why Murdaugh might have committed the murders, it opened the door for testimony about the alleged financial crimes.

The court had to leave right away on February 8 due to a bomb threat, but they later met again after several hours to continue the trial.

On February 13, Judge Newman declared that two

jurors had been discharged and substituted with new jurors due to their positive COVID-19 test results.

The jury went to the location of the killings at the request of the defense.

Following Murdaugh's 911 call, first responders on the scene served as the first prosecution witnesses.

The prosecution requested that the judge order a Snapchat employee to testify on a video that Paul Murdaugh posted just before he was killed.

The prosecution called SLED witnesses to testify on firearms and ballistics, as well as a June 21, 2021, vehicle interview with Murdaugh, during which Murdaugh described his son as, "It's really awful. I was really terrible to him" which for the jury, Waters highlighted.

The defense side argued that either "they" or "I" were being mentioned on the recording. In order to testify concerning the information Maggie's phone collected, the prosecution called an expert witness.

Two of Paul Murdaugh's closest friends were called to the stand by the prosecution to discuss their interactions with the

Murdaugh family and their conversations with Paul just before he passed away.

A witness claimed to have heard Alex's voice in a video taken by Paul just moments before the murders, according to the prosecution.

Murdaugh's former coworkers and clients were called to testify about the defendant's financial situation just before the murders took place. The prosecution claimed that stress

over the impending exposure of

Murdaugh's financial crimes served as the motive for the killings.

They also called the CEO of a local bank to testify regarding Murdaugh's embezzlement being discovered by the bank.

An expert witness was called by the prosecution, including a criminologist and a pathologist.

The prosecution called an SLED agent to testify about a timeline for the events of June 7 2021 that combined information gathered from various sources, such as cell phone tower pings, the victims' and defendant's phones, car telemetry data, and other data. A case-closing date for the prosecution was February 17.

After the prosecution rested, defense attorneys promptly called their first witness. They contacted the Colleton County coroner, who confirmed that the victim's body temperatures had only been calculated and that the recorded time of death was simply an estimate.

Buster, the defendant's son, was called to the witness stand by the defense on February 21. The defense called a number of experts, including a crime scene engineer who said that the defendant's height did not match that of the shooter and recreated the crime scene. Another expert witness stated during his testimony that he thought first responders handled the crime scene improperly.

Murdaugh entered the witness stand on February 23.

He denied killing his son and wife. Murdaugh said that he was audible on a video shot by his son at the kennels at 8:44 p.m. Before he reported discovering the bodies there later that night, Murdaugh admitted to repeatedly lying to police about whether he had been at the kennels the night of the killings.

He attributed the lies to "paranoid thinking" brought on by his opioid addiction. He also admitted stealing from legal clients and his firm, and also admitted asking a relative to shoot him (despite claiming that the shooter was unknown to him).

The same day, the prosecution's cross-examination started. The following day, Murdaugh concluded his testimony, and Judge Newman quickly dismissed the jury.

A pathologist was consulted by the defense, who felt that the state's pathologist had misidentified the entrance and exit wounds on Paul's body.

Tim Palmbach, a specialist in bloodstain spatter analysis, was also called by the defense. Palmbach has also provided testimony in well-known cases, such as the Michael Peterson trial. In his testimony, Palmbach indicated that he thought the evidence supported the presence of two shooters and that he thought a shooter would have been smeared in blood and gunshot residue. John Marvin Murdaugh, the defendant's brother, was the final witness the defense summoned.

The defense submitted a move for a directed verdict on February 27 after concluding their case, but Judge Newman rejected it.

After the defense rested their case, the prosecution said they will address the defense's arguments. On February 28, the prosecution began calling witnesses for their rebuttal case. They called four witnesses, four of whom had already testified throughout the trial. Also called to the witness stand was a police chief who had worked with Murdaugh. The last witness was a crime scene investigator who had already been questioned, and

South Carolina Attorney General Alan Wilson began the direct questioning. On February 28, the prosecution rested its response case.

On March 1, the closing arguments started.
On March 2, Judge Newman made a

statement confirming he had learned a juror had talked about the material given.

The jury member was replaced with a substitute after she was expelled for improper behavior.

The closing arguments for the state were made

by attorney Creighton Waters, and the defense was made by attorney Jim Griffin. John Meadors, an attorney for the state, made the closing argument and response.

On March 2, the jury was charged and the

deliberation process began.

The jury found Murdaugh guilty of two counts of murder and two counts of possessing a weapon during a violent crime on March 2, 2023 after deliberating for three hours.

In tense exchanges befitting the culmination of a high-stakes trial, Newman addressed Murdaugh personally and assured him that he would receive visits from the dead every night.

While you're trying to fall asleep at night, you have to see Paul and Maggie. I'm sure they stop by to see you, he said.

They did, according to Murdaugh. Yet he also argued repeatedly that he had been wrongly accused of the murders.

I'm innocent, he said.

Nonetheless, Newman mentioned Murdaugh's habit of keeping up his lies about the facts of the case.

When will it be over? asked the judge.

The judge also brought up Murdaugh's opioid addiction, which the defense tried to use to justify their client's actions. In addition to discussing his numerous encounters with Murdaugh as a lawyer in the South

Carolina court system, Newman seemed to suggest that the impact of heavy drug usage could have contributed to the killings.

"It's possible that you weren't the one who killed them. He said that it might have been the monster you've turned into.

Because cellphone video evidence revealed that Murdaugh had been at the crime scene minutes before the murders were committed, the defense's attempt to establish "reasonable doubt" was severely damaged.

Instead, the jury agreed with the prosecution's case, which mostly drew on circumstantial evidence such as phone and car monitoring systems that showed Murdaugh's activities on the night of the deaths.

The verdict was broadcast live on major broadcast and cable news networks across the United States as a result of the case's great public attention.

Judge Newman refused the defense's move for a mistrial after the verdict was announced by stating,

"The evidence of guilt is overwhelming." All of the evidence, including indirect and direct evidence, "led to one conclusion, and that's the conclusion you all reached," he told the jury.

The jury had reached a "correct conclusion as they perceived the law and facts," Newman later remarked.

On March 3, 2023, at 10:08 a.m., Murdaugh was given two consecutive life sentences without the possibility of parole.

Murdaugh was sent to the Kirkland Correctional Facility in the far Northwest side of Columbia, South Carolina.

Creighton Waters, the chief prosecutor, declared that justice had been served once the verdict was announced.

Who your family is doesn't matter, Waters remarked. "It's irrelevant how much money you actually have or how much people think you have. No matter how well-known you are, it is irrelevant. In South Carolina, justice will be served if you do wrong, break the law, or murder he said.

www.ingramcontent.com/pod-product-compliance
Lightning Source LLC
Chambersburg PA
CBHW070551220526
45467CB00003B/1163